Beneath the Surface

Paula Schorr

Sharon —
This is your T-Y.
Counselor speaking!
Love you!

Paula Schorr

Green Heart Living Press

Dedication

To my family of origin

Contents

Introduction

I inherited the storytelling gene from my mother. She spun quite a tale, comprehensively laying out the plot, sometimes sprinkling in Yiddish phrases. Inevitably she would say, "To make a long story short," which actually signaled the opposite—that the narrative would go on a while.

To make a long story short, I have enjoyed writing short stories, songs, and haiku since college. It's been a longtime dream to author a book. With retirement as a catalyst in 2008, I began to put energy into updating earlier creations and recomposing memoir material. A stage of life thing? Definitely! As I approach my seventh decade I'm looking backwards and forward. Deeply imprinted memories are crying out for expression. I must release!

These pre- and post-coming-out chapters of my life have universal purpose. Readers struggling with sexual orientation, anxiety, adolescence, and self-esteem may find solace here . . . or at least a few laughs about the herstorical "olden days." How is a lesbian made? I don't know the answer or any formulaic set of factors. I can only offer myself as a singular sample of an American woman-loving-woman. Humor plays a role in the telling. I hope to entertain the reader while testifying.

One demographic of impact is my roots as an Ashkenazi Jew who lost family members in the Holocaust. My maternal grandmother immigrated from Poland in the early 1900s. After Hitler invaded Poland in 1939, she never heard from her mother and sister again despite efforts to locate them. That year also ended with the untimely death at age thirty-nine of my maternal grandfather and namesake, Paul. These tragic legacies affected how I was reared and how I traditionally reacted to life events. Was I destined to die at thirty-nine too? Fear of the worst happening ranked as a major theme. I was taught, "Never leave your family!"

Peer pressure and lookism contributed to my struggle with my appearance and body maturation through adolescence, not an unusual circumstance. Still, I differed from the other kids. An atypical teen, I didn't rebel. I didn't confront. I caused no problems. I obeyed my curfew until I graduated high school. Most importantly, I buried my attraction to girls.

Had I not so vigorously repressed these early erotic feelings, I suspect my path would have been even more complicated. But that was not me. My over-controlling inner judge took care of that. My therapist once told me, "You have a very strong super-ego."

Beneath the Surface reveals the wheels and gears turning in my brain as I have tackled my existence. Laden with neuroses, obsessions, inhibitions, and prohibitions, I let it all hang out!

A Very Particular Friendship is a one-way love story against a background of junior high school and high school angst. Lesbian relationships were not an option in society back then. No one talked about lesbian anything, leaving me alone to process my emotions.

Bill and Me marks the beginning of my companionship with Bill, my first gay friend and a kindred soul. Entering my life during the awkward teen years, he saved me from the kinds of social stresses emanating from the straight world at school. It wasn't my intention, but it just so happened that any nosiness or possible questions about my sexuality were negated by heterosexual assumption since we were seen together a lot. He was colorful, creative, and crazy funny! May he rest in peace.

Inspection comes from an intense personal hygiene ritual that was directed almost daily by my fourth grade teacher at PS 152 Manhattan. New York City educators could be tough and demeaning to students in a way that rivaled treatment by boot camp sergeants. Inspection raised my young cortisol levels. Here was an opportunity to develop a school anxiety disorder!

Blue Nevus tells of the removal of an ominous facial mole when I was seventeen. The mole would not let go of me easily with its deep roots and my mother's attachment to it.

    Coif Formation traces the herstory of my hairstyles and their connection to my personal evolution. Culture and mood have influenced my chosen hairdos. My hair is my signature.

    Finally, *The Emergence of Rockin' Bad Paula* is a look at lesbian self-esteem and its representation by my alter-ego.

    And so I invite you to dive deep into my true being and travel beneath the surface.

Chapter 1

A Very Particular Friendship

Shannon was the best-looking and most popular girl at Linwood Junior High. Being observant, I took in this information as I acclimated to my first days at the school. It was November 1964.

I was the new kid. Each day I was learning about Linwood's social hierarchy. I was already an anxious, nail-biting child. Now, along with an increasing academic workload, I had the dreadful task of figuring out how to fit into the scene without attracting too much attention and abuse from the natives. Being the new girl in school was one of my worst fears. In seventh grade at age eleven, I transferred to Linwood Junior High School in North Brunswick, New Jersey from Junior High School 52 Manhattan. I might as well have come from a different planet. I was alien, out-of-place, a stranger. So, I channeled my nervous energy into studying my new surroundings and classmates. I wanted to fit in, feel like I belonged and pronto! Maybe I could figure it all out. Generally, this was how I responded to big changes in my life. I had difficulty accepting that I needed time to adjust, perhaps months. Even years. I was not a Zen child.

One thing was certain in junior high school— conformity reigned! I began a social re-education. Here in New Jersey it was suddenly time to grow up. As a newcomer I was a target. On my second day of school two greasers snickered at me for wearing short, white socks. Did those socks signal immaturity? I reacted quickly. By the next day I had given up wearing anklets, depositing my abundant supply into my eight-year-old sister's sock drawer. Probably okay for her to wear them a few years more.

From what I had noticed, knee socks, tights, and stockings were safe from criticism. Going from anklets to nylon stockings was too big a jump. I couldn't see that happening. I loathed dresses, anything lacy and meshy. I was not ready for the sexy garter belt and its femme implications. I had seen my mother attaching stockings to her girdle or garter belt thousands of times, and nothing about the ritual or these strange accessories appealed to me. Ultimately, I had to utilize a garter belt to wear nylons for monthly school dances. No girl wore socks to a dance! My garter belt was functional with minimal frill. Still, I bowed to peer pressure even though I felt costumed. I favored knee socks and tights for most school days. My goal was to become less conspicuous.

There were other requirements for integration and survival in the daily jungle of school besides hosiery. Seventh grade marked a point of expected body maturation. While dressing for gym in the locker room during my first week, my peripheral vision confirmed another golden rule for female students at Linwood. Every girl, no matter what her physical development, wore a brassiere. I was flat-chested and still wearing undershirts. Truth revealed itself in the bras of that locker room. I was still an outsider. Embarrassed, I huddled by the corner lockers to quickly change in and out of my gym suit, trying to hide my undergarment of childhood. I might have been the quickest changer in my gym class. This went on for a few weeks.

Puberty marked a new way of life that paralleled seventh grade. My mother wasn't eager to guide me through this stage of female development. Way behind in her mother-to-daughter discussions, we hadn't yet talked about breasts, bras and body odor. I doubted we ever would if I had to wait for her to initiate. Into my second week at school I began a nagging campaign to convince my mother to buy me a stretch bra. Several girls in gym class wore these beginner bras.

"You don't need a bra yet," she answered too quickly. She had no idea what I was facing. Technically, she was right. But, I was so tired of hiding and contorting while changing for gym. No one had noticed my undershirt yet, but the stress of potential revelation was too much. I wasn't going back to that locker room without a bra!

After pestering her non-stop I finally got my mother to drive us to E. J. Korvettes, a local department store that happened to carry stretch bras and hundreds of other useless and useful products. In the middle of the underwear section my mother studied the trainer bras like they were strange entities from a foreign culture. She still disbelieved my need. At least the size was easy enough to choose - small! This tiny, stretchy piece of material brought me the courage and proper coverage to return to the center of the locker room where I could openly change clothes and be around the buzz of my peers.

I started using deodorant after I borrowed a gym suit from one of the more popular girls and she informed me that I had stunk it up. I don't know how I survived that comment. I never even thought to bring the sweaty uniform home to wash before returning it. It never occurred to me that I had body odor. What was that? The situation required emergency action. The next day I began to use my mother's Secret spray antiperspirant before school. Soon I had my own aerosol can of Right Guard deodorant, the pervasive aroma of the girls' locker room.

I knew from gym class that females with hairy legs were a rarity at Linwood. I badgered my mother to allow me to shave my legs. She was afraid about me handling razors, fearing I would slice myself. Why? I had good manual skills. Taking matters into my own hands, I used my father's razor without asking. The next time he shaved he nicked himself because my leg and underarm hairs had dulled the blade.

He screamed at me to keep away from his stuff. Still, bearing his wrath was worth having a week or so of sleek legs.

Of course the stubble returned. Continuing to complain to my mother finally broke her down and led to a solution. She permitted me to try Nair, a cream depilatory product she regularly utilized. With victorious glee I applied it on the night of my first school dance. I spread the cream on my legs and waited. Then I wiped off my legs until they were clean and smooth. Success! Liberation! But there was only one problem that I didn't discover until the dance. Nair left a mild, fishy odor. I should have showered after removing the leg hair. The essence permeated my stockings. I could detect the smell intermittently as I moved around and socialized in the school gym. I don't know if anyone else noticed. I may have looked happy as I danced the chicken-back, swim, and shimmy with the other teens and a slow dance with a short, skinny kid named Manny, but the whiffs of Nair from my legs tortured me all night.

Back on my first day at Linwood Junior High the guidance counselor assigned me a companion, Janis, to help navigate my virgin voyage around the two-story building. Janis kindly invited me to her lunch table in the cafeteria, and I met her circle of friends. The group became a temporary anchor for me. They were the smart, well-behaved students, the kind whom teachers adored, the kind who weren't focusing on boys yet. Of course, my grandmother was thrilled when I told her one girl's last name was "Levine." That meant that there were Jews in North Brunswick after all. I could pass for one of those good girls myself, but I also yearned for something else to perk up my life. Without my nest of old friends from New York City, things were depressing.

From my bench in the cafeteria with the good girls, I often scanned the other tables in the lunchroom. Following the guffaws and explosive merriment, my eyes found the in-crowd. Shannon habitually sat in that section with an animated crew of boys and girls bouncing around her, following her every word. She seemed to mesmerize them with her laughter, chic hairstyle, beautiful smiling face and dominating presence.

The in-crowd seemed anything but boring. Action! Life was happening there at her table! I'd seen these different personalities strutting around the halls between classes. They swaggered with their nobility. These were the school celebrities: best dressed and most attractive. Some were couples going steady. There were guys from the baseball and basketball teams holding hands with girls who were cheerleaders.

Shannon herself was a cheerleader. But she was more. Her vibes traveled, wafted over the lunchroom and transfixed me. Half-daydreaming, I decided I could be her devotee too. Better, I wondered how it would feel to be part of her clique or to be her good friend.

As I adjusted to the seventh grade, I had a quiet social life. Although I was expanding my school and home friendship networks, I hadn't bonded closely with anyone or found my niche yet. I remained in a kind of limbo. It took another year for circumstances to alter. In eighth grade, the two academically advanced classes were reshuffled, re-alphabetized, and resized. I ended up in Shannon's class, the bottom half of the alphabet. What precious luck!

By now I had joined Linwood, hygiene intact: shaved (finally got an electric razor) and deodorized armpits, hairless legs, and frizzy hair under control. An increased inventory of knee socks and tights complemented my "mix and match" arrangements of shifts, skirts, jumpers, blouses, and sweaters. All systems were go. Now it was all about Shannon.

The process of getting to know her began the first day of eighth grade. Each subject was taught in a different classroom with voluntary seating. This offered many possibilities to place myself near Shannon. What a fun game. In six different classrooms I deposited myself in Shannon's zone, near to, but not right next to her. There had to be the appearance of randomness in how I chose my spot. I didn't want to seem obvious, pushy, or stalking. Of course, no one was keeping tabs on my seating choices except for my strict inner judge: why go through so many considerations to pick a damn seat? I wanted to be close enough to Shannon to pass notes or be heard quietly mocking the teacher. I wondered if there was a science or master plan to initiating a "particular friendship?"[1]

---

[1] Interestingly, the phrase "particular friendship" refers to close, intimate, and forbidden relationships between nuns inside the convent.

The truth was that I fell for Shannon right away. My heart fluttered and thumped when I saw her each morning at school. Knowing we had six classes together thrilled me. I was getting hooked on Shannon with regular doses. I felt intoxicated and captivated, but also intensely nervous and frightened. Underneath it all, I knew these were not just friendship feelings. At the same time my mind worked overtime to quash any condemning sexual feelings. I put locks and chains on my desire. I policed myself, attempting to banish the tantalizing thoughts.

Yet my secret physical attraction seeped out in other ways. My self deprecating sense of humor captured her attention. This was an important way to connect because I had no boyfriend about whom to converse, giggle, or compare notes. Also, I didn't use cosmetics, which eliminated the girl alliances that formed in front of lavatory mirrors in between classes or at the end of gym. So, I entertained.

I passed witty notes in class. If Shannon laughed, I felt high. I drew futuristic caricatures and cartoons of Shannon, me, and a few other female classmates in careers as surgeon, psychiatrist, ballerina, artist, lawyer. We would share a professional building, which I also sketched and decorated with advertisements describing our services. I was hatching my own little family through these doodling fantasies, another way of saying, "Let's stay together forever."

Halfway into eighth grade a wish came true. Shannon invited me to her lunch table. Without a goodbye, I left the good girls, a sudden graceless shift on my part. But now there was ascension! I joined the royal inner circle. Popular kids now knew who I was and greeted me in the halls. My social status went up a few degrees, but there was some associated stress with my success. Just as with Shannon, I played court jester to her entourage. I felt safest as a jokester. I didn't have to reveal too much about myself that way. Humor was a decoy to potential questions like— what's your favorite lipstick shade or do you have a boy-friend?

One place I felt less guarded about my attraction to Shannon was in the realm of Linwood girls' softball. The camaraderie on our team pulled us closer. We loved battling our opponents. We were athletic and enjoyed competition. We got dirty together. We hugged after victories. I defended at second base, Shannon covered first. We turned double plays. This was physicality that I could openly embrace. We grooved! Shannon was a reliable fielder and masterful batter of doubles and triples. A card-carrying tomboy, I hit mostly singles, but had a respectable throwing arm and could've been considered a golden-glover.

Within the bounds of the game I could publicly express my absolute adoration and passion for Shannon under the camouflage of, "Beautiful hit!" or "Unbelievable catch!" as my eyes feasted on her tanned and well-muscled body in motion. She could do no wrong. She was the top of the top, the peak of the peak at Linwood: a talented jock, a pretty prom princess, captain of the cheerleaders, a fashion trend-setter, a straight-A student. Shannon towered!

I also idealized and idolized Shannon's family: financially well-off transplants from Dallas, Texas. I viewed them as southwestern aristocracy. They lived in a large split-level home in a neighborhood of similar dwellings. Only the sparkling black presidential Lincoln Continental and powder-blue Ford Thunderbird convertible in the widened driveway hinted at the abundance within.

The amenities of Shannon's home surpassed mine by light years. A cornucopia of goodies greeted hungry teenagers who visited. Need I add: there were no rules about snacking. Shannon's mother never interfered. She was often elsewhere in the home when I was over. Wherever she was seemed miles away... like Texas.

How unlike my home. When I had friends at my house, which was rare, the atmosphere was notably different. My grandmother walked slowly up the stairs into the kitchen to stare at me and my friends and ascertain what and how much we were eating. Even if her food monitoring was a legacy of the Depression, more importantly, she was making sure that I didn't ruin my appetite for dinner at six. My mother and grandmother were quite emphatic and stern about our dinner ritual.

Shannon and her older sister, Diane, enjoyed me, "Pah-la," as they called me in their sweet southern accents. I was an anomaly: the skinny, humorous, Jewish girl from New Yawk City. I intrigued the WASPs, with my otherness. Diane sometimes drove us wildly around the back roads of

Princeton in the Lincoln Continental, topping off the rides with stops at Buxton's ice cream restaurant. What teen wouldn't drool at that? I had my first hoagie sandwich at their house after school one day, and I devoured it, crossing hungrily into goy gastro-culture. Eating ham and dairy together in a sandwich? For a kosher kid like me, this ranked as subversive and sinful.

Still, there was another problem about ingesting the ham, lettuce, and cheese, and it had nothing to do with pork and Judaism. I knew my mother would harass me if I didn't eat supper with my family at six. What was so bad about eating a sandwich at a friend's house or stopping for ice cream and skipping dinner? It certainly wasn't frequent. The dinnertime issue was a serious edict, the violation of which resulted in being tormented with guilt inflicted by my mother and her mother. The matriarchs had their own rigid rules and levels of tolerance. Sitting at the dinner table with the family was a must. In contrast, Shannon's house was a haven where life was freer. I was too embarrassed to refuse the hoagie because of my mother and grandmother's inflexibility around family routine. I didn't want to admit that to anyone! From another viewpoint, I was thirteen and beginning to leave the nest. Did eating this hoagie symbolically mark a point of rebellion, a declaration of independence? It certainly expanded my culinary repertoire. Hoagies, heroes, sub sandwiches became my guilty pleasure.

My mother grew increasingly jealous and threatened by my repeated lateness for dinner. She interpreted my behavior as a slight to her and the family. The time between 5:45 and 6:00 pm became both agony and a whirlwind as I reluctantly left Shannon's house and raced down the street. I generally waited until the last minute to go. Sometimes that was 5:59 pm because I couldn't tear myself away from Shannon and her household. Yet, how could I possibly make it home on time? Shannon and Diane found my exits laughable. As I revved up to leave, the sisters playfully teased and taunted me, guessing at my upcoming punishment. Their banter pleased me enough to face the inevitable sentence for tardiness.

I was a martyr for love. True, I never really apportioned the proper time to cover the mile back home, which included traversing a housing development, crossing Route 1 at rush hour, and cutting through a drive-in and small park. The finish line of this marathon race was always grim. My mother glared at me, her silence matched by a stricken look on my grandmother's face. She assumed I was dead if I was not home on time—a Holocaust legacy. These were my consequences: no yelling, no grounding, I just had to endure the suffering matriarchs, sit down and eat dinner. Guilt for dessert.

My mother feared that I was being seduced by the opulence of Shannon's lifestyle. Who wouldn't be? The first time my mother saw the shiny Lincoln Continental was at a school function. It made an impression on her. The vehicle stood out as the undisputed king of the parking lot. I was well aware that we were working class and struggling while

Shannon's family shopped at Saks Fifth Avenue and drove limos.

I never hounded my parents about money or material items. I had what I needed. But I could dream, couldn't I? No matter, my mother was insecure. She acted as though in competition with Shannon. She wanted me to show more open appreciation for our family. How? Always stay home? Only talk about my parents and sister? Only have friends who were on the same economic level? Or were Jewish? My mother was wary of this cross-class friendship; I was compelled by it.

I had my first sleepover at Shannon's during the winter holiday of ninth grade. I was overjoyed but also anxious about this next step in our friendship. I was so afraid of my attraction. To me, the sleepover was a pinnacle. Had Shannon just been a friend, I could have relaxed and been spontaneous. But I was living in another dimension. I was enthralled. I remember exactly what we did that evening. We danced to the Doors and Laura Nyro, line-danced to Motown, sang with Donovan, snacked on Judaically-forbidden foods, drank Pepsi, watched TV, and stayed up real late. Euphoric, I was on a secret roller-coaster and so far surviving.

Then came the nerve-wracking climax of the evening, that most desired and feared event: bedtime. No question, I would change to pajamas in the bathroom. I was modest and embarrassed about that. In my own made-up formula of time, I figured Shannon would simultaneously change clothes in her bedroom. If my calculation was correct, I wouldn't ever have to see her even partially disrobed. I craved to look at her, but I couldn't let myself. God, was I nervous! Self-restraint went into overdrive. There were unspoken borders for me to patrol while lying horizontally. Blocking out Shannon, I took restriction to bed instead.

I was familiar with restricting myself. I did this in my family all of the time. I crawled and curled over as close as possible to the edge of the mattress whose comfort and spaciousness I would not get to enjoy. I lay turned away from Shannon and against the wall. How natural was that? She must have thought me bizarre. My poor overactive mind. When I woke up the next morning it appeared I had either exercised great control or had become a statue while sleeping. Rising from the bed, it was hard to move because my body had been confined, frozen, and cramped in the same position all night. Secret love and perfect devotion were physically taxing.

The morning after, my mother came to pick me up. I'm sure she was uneasy about entering the higher-class domain she perceived as the rival for my loyalty. Shannon and I were in her bedroom, me packing my stuff to the background beat of a Rolling Stones song when my mother and Shannon's mother came in. It was before this audience that my mother made her move.

"Paula, did you tell Shannon what you got for Chanukah?"

My head spun around in disbelief. Shannon turned

the music down. Why suddenly raise this question? Was she really doing this? I understood that she wanted to prove something, but this was awkward. As much as I wanted to scream at her, I had never verbally defied my mother. Instead, I cringed, I shrunk. She ordered and I complied.

"Tell Shannon what you got for Chanukah!"

Time stood still. All awaited my reply. I obeyed the command. Sheepishly, I mumbled, "An electric typewriter."

I blocked out everyone's reactions, if there were any, and I think there were. I knew my mother was demonstrating that my family gave expensive gifts too. She must have believed I would brag about the typewriter, and everyone would realize something or other that would make her the winner of my affections. I sincerely appreciated receiving the typewriter, a special and modern present, but it never figured as a major topic of conversation between me and friends. Still, my mother acted as if she had gained some edge in the class wars. All I wanted to do was go home to my single bed.

Shannon told me the following story several weeks after my overnight. She had invited our classmate, Danielle, to sleep over. Danielle stood out as a young hippy who wore Indian-print dresses: ahead of her time and definitely not mainstream. She read Herman Hesse. Sarcastic, contemptuous, and a little arrogant, she fancied herself an outcast. Yet, she was not rebellious or a discipline problem in school. She wasn't hung up on peer acceptance either. She was pretty unique and that's what drew some of us to her.

Shannon confided that Danielle had tried to touch her while they were in bed. Shannon stopped Danielle, I don't know how, and that was that! I was astonished and taken aback by Danielle's fearless attempt. Danielle didn't control her desires. Her behavior was unimaginable to me, but our yearnings for Shannon were the same. Danielle followed her instincts while I pinioned mine in the corner of Shannon's bed. Interestingly, I noticed no obvious changes in how Shannon subsequently dealt with Danielle other than no further overnights. It seemed the repercussions from this incident occurred more in my mind than reality. I now worried that Danielle had opened up Pandora's box and given Shannon new detective skills.

There was a second disturbing incident between Shannon and Danielle that year. Danielle's attraction took a stealthy and insidious turn. Our English class was putting on a production of West Side Story. Shannon played the part of the mature, passionate, and sensual Anita. I had a crush on Anita too. The male roles in the play outnumbered the females, so Danielle became a member of the Jets gang. I played Anybodys, a Jet, a street waif, a tomboy, a likely future lesbian.

In one scene the Jets push Anita around and treat her roughly when she appears at Doc's drugstore to deliver a secret message from Maria to Tony. During the confrontation Anita is molested by the Jets. It's an ugly mob interaction that grows more animalistic by the moment. During one of our practices, Danielle, a Jet, pawed and stroked Shannon's body in a totally non-fictional way. Only Shannon and Danielle knew what occurred. No one else noticed.

When Shannon described this encounter to me, my admiration for Danielle's honesty, guts, and individuality ceased. Her behavior was dark, devious, out of control, and forcible. She made me paranoid. On the one hand, I didn't have to worry further about competing with Danielle for Shannon's attention. Still, I wondered if the brilliant and disturbing Danielle could "read" me. Would she blow my cover? Then what? This was definitely something to obsess about in my spare time.

My mother continued to be an obstacle to how much time Shannon and I shared outside of school. I had already spent two sleepovers at Shannon's. My mother looked angry and hurt when I queried about another overnight. Her body language and attitude translated into an emphatic "No!" She answered unsympathetically,

"Weren't you just there last weekend?"

So what if that was true? Shannon regularly invited me over. I used to lie and tell her I was busy so I could avoid the process of asking my mother and enduring the inevitable backlash.

I never fought back with my mother. I never challenged her decision making. But, sometimes I thought I could read her mind. So, of course without discussing, I came up with a plan which I felt was fair and might meet her approval. I would purposely wait a number of weeks and put in some good time at home before seeking permission to stay at Shannon's again. That meant literally spending time in the house and not going off with friends. It didn't matter if I was in my room most of the time as long as I was physically in the house and close to the family. This is what seemed to matter to the matriarchs. During that interlude, I believed my mother would see that I was a loyal family member, who didn't leave home every weekend. She would recall that I was an A student and not a behavior problem. She would consider the evidence. She would have an epiphany. I finally asked for an overnight at Shannon's nearly a month later. My hopes fizzled as I watched my mother's good mood evaporate. The plan was just my own wishful thinking. Apparently, she hadn't experienced any enlightenment during my sleepover hiatus.

With the pain and ire of fresh betrayal, she said, "Don't you love your family?"

What? Her reply threw me across the room. Oh, my God! A tidal wave of guilt was coming to pull me under. The sacrificial passage of weeks since my last sleepover meant nothing as a good faith compromise. The situation was black and white. If I really loved my family, I would stay home...forever! But, no other family members were griping about me not loving them. Still, as effective as a headlock, my mother emotionally wrestled me into a double-bind. She floored me. She out-maneuvered me. She pinned me. I didn't ask for an overnight at Shannon's again. Ever.

The coup de grace to my relationship with Shannon,

however, came unexpectedly one day in the second semester of ninth grade. We had just arrived in Latin class where we sat next to each other. This was the last period of the day. The teacher was puttering around her desk and everyone was chatting. My guard was down. It was an ordinary moment like countless others in the school day. Shannon asked me a simple question. "Do you like me like a boy?"

I heard myself quickly and loudly assert "NO!" (although a lie-detector test would have nailed me.) Shannon's words set off a crescendo of alarms, alerts, and fireworks inside me. That NO! shot out of my mouth like a pre-programmed Minuteman missile from a Nevada silo, honing in on and destroying the insightful question in a counterattack. I HAD to show Shannon how absurd her inquiry was. And then, we needed to get off this topic very quickly.

In the midst of my mental crossfire I considered the conflicting messages I was sending. There was too much protest in my response. It felt like overkill. So, in an attempt to offset my over-reaction, I tried to compose myself and act normal. Could I keep my face from turning redder and return to a calm demeanor where I acted like nothing major had just occurred between us? Was it humanly possible? How could I even expect to do this? Actually, my memory is blocked on what transpired the rest of that day. I was in shock. I couldn't concentrate. Shannon had verbalized my secret and the universe heard.

The topic never again arose between us, but it was a really uncomfortable turning point. I began to untie my connection to Shannon after her recognition of my attraction. Even though I'd replied to her astute question negatively and emphatically, I didn't know how to adjust to the new territory uncovered. I started to distance myself, a silent and solo breakup known to no one but me. I acted and ached alone.

In my family we never talked out our feelings. I learned early that upsetting my mother could lead to her sudden illness. How could I explain my situation without contributing to a family crisis? My mother's blood pressure would skyrocket upon learning the news that I liked girls like boys. So, I hid my loss, a well developed habit by now. I didn't cry or rage or show the world I was miserable. Not to Shannon, not to my mother, not to anyone.

But there was, thank goodness, a reprieve right after ninth grade ended. I went to summer camp, and spent nine weeks in a country environment hundreds of miles away in upstate New York. Was it camp or love rehab? There was something to be said for distance and focusing on girl-bonding and athletics. I already had close friends at camp. Girls were more affectionate there and walked around holding hands. Girls had crushes on each other or their counselors. We were like a bunch of sisters. No one cared. No one judged. It was all platonic and safe. Life at camp distracted me and soothed my heart.

With the summer's end, I had to face my first year at New Brunswick High School and see Shannon again. Formidable hurdles, I wondered what effect each would have on me. Academically, I wasn't worried. But, it had been three months since "the question," my last reference point of our friendship. Could I just go on and pretend it never happened? That's what we did in my family. Would she be on the same wavelength? Would I have to avoid her for my own well-being? My mind was already off to the races, not a good sign.

But, before I could possibly regain my equilibrium, things changed abruptly in our geographic situation. After barely a month in tenth grade Shannon's parents transferred her to Princeton to a private, predominantly white, religious high school run by nuns. For wealthy Republicans from the South, this conservative educational milieu fit them better than the racially-mixed population at New Brunswick High School. I was disappointed in the dream family whom I'd previously idealized. Racism and classism hid behind their friendly southern smiles. However, I came to believe the transfer was a sign from above, a cosmic aid even if I didn't seek it, because it saved me from having to worry daily about encountering Shannon.

I also hadn't shaken off my self-consciousness about phoning her. Once she transferred I became passive about contact. Shannon wasn't calling me either. Adjusting to her new school and social life, I told myself.

My feelings were so discombobulated. As time passed it became emotionally easier and less complicated to find out about her life second hand through the grapevine. I practiced detachment. When one doesn't water a plant, it withers, which was the approach I took. Don't feed it and it will die.

During my senior year in high school I heard that Shannon and her new (best) friend, Liz, a Princeton schoolmate, opened a hippy boutique in New Brunswick with the help of their moneyed fathers. I never went to their store even though I spent plenty of time in downtown New Brunswick and sported hippy fashion. What stopped me? On the one hand, I missed that body-jolting chemistry of attraction, the total buzz and excitement upon seeing and being near Shannon. But, that would reactivate my hopeless longing, heartache, and all the craziness in my brain. This was my predicament. I was stuck. Seeing no other way to control or solve this eternal dilemma, I advised myself to follow an even stricter path of subtracting Shannon.

Years passed. Now I was majoring in history at Douglass College. That I ended up at this all-women's institution I attribute purely to fate. In fact, I'd begged my parents to send me to NYU. I was pushing for a co-ed school in some twisted reaction to knowing deep down that I was attracted to women. The evidence was convincing and hard to deny. I hadn't dated a soul during high school, and never attended a junior or senior prom. I didn't care that I didn't have a boyfriend. I certainly had no desire to kiss a boy or be physical. I was completely inexperienced in relationships other than with my friends and family. So, I thought a co-ed college would be a practical last-ditch effort to heterosexually influence me, to tip the scales back.

I really wanted to get away and expand my radius from the household. But, the out-of-state schools where I was accepted weren't economically viable for my parents. Trapped by their finances, my choices were extremely limited. That was why, reluctantly, I surrendered to the very local and monetarily reasonable Douglass College. I wondered if I'd ever date or marry.

I matriculated in 1970. It was exactly the right place and time, although I didn't realize it right away. As it turned out, Douglass College planted the seeds of my woman-loving selfhood, then nurtured and percolated me during a period the campus was alive with liberation: women, gay, black, latino. This was no mainstream territory. As a freshman, I remember gasping the first time I saw a lesbian couple walking around the student center holding hands unafraid. I was also initially shocked when I witnessed male and female same-sex couples making out at a women's liberation dance. No secrets, no hiding...hmm, reality was broadening.

In my senior year at Douglass I found out through the grapevine that Shannon's family had moved back to Dallas. Shannon was now attending Southern Methodist University. I can't remember how I got her phone number, but I'm sure I was as persistent as I had been in eighth grade. After five or more years of no contact, I was finally ready to phone Shannon, although not without trepidation. I needed some assistance. That aid came from a not-so-fancy cocktail of 80 proof Smirnoff vodka, Tang, and good old New Brunswick tap water, my student budget version of a screwdriver. This was the reconnection concoction.

Nursing my first drink, I dialed. I waited to hear Shannon, my heart beating like a fast metronome. Stirs of eros. A very perky voice answered the phone with a cheerful greeting. The sound of that Texan accent... I was vulnerable to that voice and all she had said was, "Hello."

"Hi, it's your old friend, Paula. How are you doing?" Her immediate response to me was surprised, but also happy and delighted. I guess I didn't have to worry about how she'd react, even though I'd basically tracked her down like a private investigator. She was laughing and saying she couldn't believe I called, and then she laughed more which exhilarated me like a quick-acting stimulant drug. Simultaneously, I was feeling the Tang cocktail's buzz and warming effects. Liking the sensations, I poured my second drink.

Whatever we were conversing about, and I can't remember exactly, Shannon sounded euphoric, giddy and giggly, almost as though she was the slightly intoxicated one. Could she be that charged up about my call? But then she revealed the latest deep development in her life, unveiling the reason for her effervescent mood. She had joined a religious sect, the Holy Order of Mans. The Holy Order of Mans? Was that supposed to be the possessive form of "man?" Poor grammar irked me. The name made no sense. I had never heard of this fringe group.

Shannon went on to say that she now had a new

name, Sister Elizabeth. Stationed at a local convent in Chicago, Sister Elizabeth was a novice. She wore a habit. As per her new vocation and lack of seniority, she was in charge of cleaning the living quarters and washing dishes. She sounded like she was prospering in her lowly status. She was in a state of non-stop joyfulness punctuated by religious rituals in her daily routine.

Wow! This was completely unexpected. Shannon was either revolutionary or a nut. I was fascinated by this strange metamorphosis: prom princess-turned-nun. This was a revolt against her upper-class rearing, not to mention her formerly chic fashion sense. Had she experienced a breakdown or an incredible breakthrough? Was this some kind of calling? I'll bet Sister Elizabeth was the most charismatic nun this sect ever had. Was she modeling after the nuns at her Princeton high school? There were so many questions, but, of course, as per her station, she could not stay on the phone forever. She had duties and obligations, and needed to prepare for Vespers. Although I couldn't picture myself ever joining a spiritual splinter group or cult, I admired her choice...because my crush on her was everlasting. I had faith in Shannon.

1973 was a life-changing year. We both majorly altered our statuses. Shannon became a nun during the winter and I came out as a lesbian in the spring. It had taken me years of hiding, discovering, denying, considering, facing, and finally accepting my sexual orientation. Shannon was the original trigger of my sexual yearnings. Though I

Beneath the Surface

suppressed those feelings, they ultimately led me to this core truth about myself.

Shannon is iconic to me. She was the precursor to my lesbianism. She was my first...and she wasn't. Now, she appears in dreams from time to time. The plots are similar. I am turned-on, hot, and ready to sleep with her. She is enticing, promising, there's a bed, but we never consummate. Apparently, the closest I can come is internalizing her. As such, I am grateful.

36

Chapter 2

Bill & Me

I met Bill during junior high school in 1966 when our families moved into the newly constructed, suburban North Brunswick Village, its streets (except for mine) named after the early astronauts. Bill lived on (Alan) Shepard Avenue. He had relocated from Maryland with his mother and older brother after his parents divorced. In my small, sheltered world I didn't have any friends from divorced families, and I was curious what it was like. He introduced himself as "Bill" but declared his birth name was "William Obey Toddard Schafer." I thought—who had that many names other than royalty (or my parakeet, Antunny Yeagle Baruch Budgerigar Toenail Schorr aka "Tunny").

I initially thought Bill was embellishing his origins. Or maybe I was jealous. He claimed a predominantly Mediterranean lineage with roots in Spain, France, Germany and possibly Italy. His genealogy was exotic and multi-culti, more exciting than my near one hundred percent Ash-kenazi Jewish DNA.

Regarding Bill's family tree, I regret that I never met his father, a compelling missing piece in his story. Bill never discussed his parents' divorce or his father, not that we talked about serious things back then. The thing is, I'm not sure if his father maintained a steady relationship with him. Never saw a picture of the man. Heard he was short and balding. "Schafer," the man with the German DNA, I presumed. But, Bill's mother certainly made her colorful presence known. Named Aida after Verdi's captive Ethiopian princess, she was a striking, alluring, desirable brunette. She gave off the air of being cultured. An olive-skinned woman, I believed her bloodline was the source of the spice in Bill's genes.

After hanging out at Bill's house long enough, I also found Aida to be overly dramatic and emotional. She was a high-maintenance diva whose behavior was tinged with hysteria. Aida had a lover perhaps twenty years younger, Andy, a dark-haired, bearded, hunky, handsome operatic tenor. When I was visiting, Andy often serenaded her around the house, probably to calm and pacify her. Aida could be volatile. Often, she screamed at Bill. Or maybe that was just her way of communicating.

One time we were stoned in Bill's bedroom, watching, imitating, and mocking soap opera characters on TV. We spent a lot of time deriding life, people and things. Our mutual hobby. Everything and everyone was absurd and laughable, especially mainstream culture. Pot frequently enhanced our time together, and in this case, it certainly intensified Aida's interruption of our sarcasm session.

"Billy!" she called him at a high volume right outside the door, a shrill, trilling voice as though she had a foreign accent, but she didn't. I loved that she called him Billy—it was cute and personal, but she was no opera singer.

"Feed the dogs!" she shrieked. The dogs were two pedigreed Afghans, long haired, regal, and also high-strung. Aida's shouts stirred them up. They moved simultaneously. Their toenails clicked on the wooden floors as they scrambled and slid around the uncarpeted bi-level house. Bill and Aida resembled those dogs: Bill more for his locks and style and his mother for her beauty and excitable nature.

"I know! Go away!" he yelled loudly through the closed door. She constantly irritated him, you could tell. They bickered when they had to converse, but from my viewpoint, she seemed otherwise unconcerned about Bill's activities. Whether or not accurate, I felt that Bill's experiences of parental control and discipline were the opposite of mine. I'd never considered responding to my mother so dismissively, and I doubt she would have accepted such disrespect.

My mother and grandmother imposed rules on me rooted in Holocaust trauma. The regulations could be summarized under the main decree: Don't leave home! And if you have to, don't go too far or for too long! A good-girl-firstborn daughter, ever-striving to please, I submitted. I was always waiting for a reward for my compliance, such as more freedom, but it never materialized, not even on the night of my high school graduation when I requested a later curfew. Could a National Honor Society kid get a break? No amount of achievements bought me liberty. Not under the mother's governance. (I actually broke the curfew and returned home after three in the morning. This was one of the rare times I created my own justice. It shock-waved my parents, but I don't recall being punished.)

However, Bill was mostly unrestrained as young males commonly were. I never noticed him rushing to be home at a particular time. Rather, Bill lived in the moment and "'til the break of dawn" if he so desired.

Bill, as noted, carried himself with the glamour of an Afghan. He was quite handsome, and could've modeled. With his appealing soccer-player's tanned physique, he stood five feet eleven with brown curls, a young Adonis. (He once showed me how to maximize my curls by rubbing a smidge of baby oil in my hair. Those were the pre-gel days.) Au courant in fashion, he owned a look that separated him from the popular high school guys, the jocks, with their signature Converse sneakers, T-shirts, and jeans. Besides Bill's curly hair, I really dug his attire. A long-term tomboy, I always noticed men's clothes. I coveted many of Bill's shoes, especially the brown, wing-tipped loafers with the buckles. Clunky and funky. I fell in love with those shoes, and imagined myself wearing them.

Bill danced incredibly as if he'd been born and raised to a funky soul beat. When we went to the monthly high school dances, he was a wanted man. I lost him as soon as we hit the gymnasium. The Black girls corralled Bill for themselves while I watched proudly and a bit enviously. I was no wallflower. I wanted to dance with him! Few white boys could move like him. Fine as he was though, no girl could ever lasso him because Bill was attracted to men.

Nevertheless, Bill and I hung out so much that some school peers thought we were a couple. That worked for me, because I had no urge to date boys. Aside from the fact that I was modest, I had no desire to tongue-kiss or get felt up as was the path and desire of most of my female peers, or so I believed. The thought of dating made me quite nervous. I didn't want any male sexually, although aesthetically I appreciated well-developed arms and legs.

I was drawn to Bill, loved him, admired his fit body, but I never wanted to sleep with him. Our relationship was completely platonic, which brought me a sense of safety and freedom to be myself. Bill and I acted ridiculously, playfully, often speaking publicly to each other in munchkin voices. We totally amused ourselves.

I loved that his sense of humor and mine converged in oddball ways. We would break into munchkin anywhere, munchkin as a second language. We definitely qualified as non-conformists, outsiders, maybe even weirdos compared to the general high school population. We had our own version of attending the prom.

Prom night in the late 1960s: a super-straight, all-American life stage event to which every girl dreamed of being asked. I'd internalized that message even as a tomboy. Despite my feelings about young males, I felt some sadness at prom time, knowing, feeling that I would never be asked. And I never was, a seasonal blow to my ego and latent femininity. The prom was about being chosen by the opposite sex, a rehearsal for adulthood. By going to the prom one earned a female badge of achievement. I never fit into this particular life plan.

But, if I'd ever actually been asked, I would have dreaded attending. That level of anticipatory anxiety and apprehension overcame me once. A casual friend mentioned that this guy, Tony, who sat at our lunch table, might ask me to the senior prom. Tony had straight black hair, was totally good-looking, popular enough, and his legs were muscular—yes, I'd seen him in his gym shorts.

I'd never dated anyone, much less have the first date be prom night. This possibility set off alarms about having to wear formal attire, make-up, and experience potential physical intimacy with my date. Wasn't that bound to happen? As a grateful date I'd have to at least kiss him. For some reason, I felt I had no power in this scenario, no choice, I'd have to submit. According to stories I'd heard, I could probably count on getting drunk. Then I wouldn't care what happened. Not a pretty resolution, but in my head the best possible outcome.

I admit the idea that Tony was interested flattered

me momentarily...well maybe for a day. Then I began to pray that he wouldn't ask. I barely knew him. We sat diagonally across the lunch table, that's all. We'd never talked one-on-one. I had no urge to engage him in conversation to break the ice further. I didn't know how to pretend to be an average, flirtatious teenage girl hoping to be asked to the prom. Such a girl would not have cringed at the thought of crinolines. Heels, even tiny ones, wouldn't frighten her.

Ultimately, after a few weeks, Tony had not asked. The prom came and went. My worries instantly evaporated, replaced by a feeling of rejection in my gut...I was clearly lacking in some way. Still, a greater sense of relief won out, the pressure off.

How did Bill and I honor this alleged apex of school social events? What was the proper course of action? On prom night we situated ourselves on a curb outside the back of our high school, near the parking lot. We watched the couples disembark from their vehicles and limos, and sashay along the decrepit concrete pathway to a transformed dreamworld inside the building, the land I would never know. From our stoop, we freely analyzed and criticized the procession, though more personalities than outfits. The white couples, subdued in pastels, resembled fairy tale beings stiffly heading to the ball. The black couples showed up in more varied and brilliant colors that screamed upbeat celebration.

My sidewalk runway commentary focused on particular white girls. "That bitch cheerleader called my hair frizzy last week. Look at hers! Is that plastic? Too much hairspray, looks like a helmet. Actually, she resembles a doll. Not a friendly doll, either. Like one I watched on *The Twilight Zone.* That one getting out of the station wagon now—she looks so innocent, but she's a greaser with a vicious temper. We're all scared of her in homeroom." A few weeks before when I was gathering info for the yearbook, she'd proudly told me her nickname.

"Gary calls me Lover," I repeated this tidbit in munchkin. She had scratched Gary's name on her arm with a safety pin.

"She likes to fight. I always say hello to her, though, I'm not stupid."

Because of my long-term affinity for menswear, I found less to criticize among the male dates. As a child, I enjoyed wearing my father's ties and perfecting different knots much more than other dress-ups. This entertained me for hours in front of the mirror and contributed to the early development of an alter-ego, the businessman, Mr. Hunter. Birthed when I was five or six, he always dressed in a jacket and tie. Clearly, my own dressing history interfered with a balanced evaluation of the boys.

Sitting on the curb, our "orchestra seats," Bill and I dressed to express the polarities of the evening, us versus them. Bill wore cut-offs and a tee shirt. Falling on the other end of the gender attire spectrum, I wore my father's oversized army shorts, belted to stay up, and a baggy tee shirt as flowing as the Cinderella gowns parading by. I felt so damn comfortable! My mother had been appalled that I would wear those large men's shorts out of the house. I could see it in her face that evening, but she made no attempt to stop me. Whatever I did at that point of my life that she didn't comprehend, she chalked up to my being a hippy. That's what they called us at school too—hippies! With a little disdain. Because they didn't understand us.

I know my mother always wished I'd had a boyfriend, but thankfully she wasn't at all aggressive about imposing that on me. She happened not to be an assertive, invasive, questioning Jewish mother. But her silence also held impactful messages. She didn't necessarily seek or want to know the truth. I put out vibes that I didn't want to talk about boyfriends, and she received them. All without us ever murmuring a word. But, I will not forget the disappointment that flickered across her face when I told her Bill was not my boyfriend, but a good friend. (Secretly, she hoped any male she ever saw me with was my boyfriend. I had to smash her hopes and dreams a few times.) My father simply said, "He's a fairy!"

"He is not!!" I replied defensively, though of course he was correct. Denial was the safest and quickest way to end this conversation. My mother glared at my father for bringing up such a taboo topic. My father had made his assessment quickly after meeting Bill for no more than five minutes in our driveway while watering the lawn, all the time needed for his macho pronouncement.

The few times my father had made cracks about homosexuals at home, it would trigger my mother. Sometimes he did it on purpose, cruelly believing it was funny. This subject matter was not to be discussed or joked about! At random times in the past at the dinner table I heard my father refer to a former high school English teacher as a lesbian, and it drove my mother crazy. Especially that he actually used the word, lesbian, which was akin to profanity, I guessed.

My mother stood up for the teacher vehemently, "She was not!!" Sound familiar? I wonder if my mother was subconsciously prescient of my future lesbianism, the reason she never pushed exploring my "no boyfriend" status.

During high school, a pattern developed on weekends when a bunch of us were out at local gatherings or parties. Bill would suddenly disappear around 11 pm or so, failing to say goodbye, even to whoever had transported him. He was so slick. Not that I was spying, but I never saw him exit or prepare to leave. The whole thing mimicked a magic act where Bill was both the magician and the vanishing object. Now you see him, now you don't. Or maybe it was like Clark Kent changing into Superman. No one ever witnessed the transition. At some point we would say, "Where's Bill?" Then, after scanning the area and feeling puzzled, we would conclude that he'd left.

This process happened weekly when we hung out. The recurring evanescence annoyed me, as if he needed to escape from us. I finally figured out that he was slipping away to take the bus or train to New York City to his gay world, which livened after midnight. For some reason his departure had to be mysterious.

There was a club song back in the early '70s, *Follow the Wind*, by the Midnight Movers. I considered that tune Bill's anthem, and I always think of him when I play it. The words repeated to a primal, funky beat, accompanied by a super horn riff and driving guitars. Bill rocked that message. Really, you couldn't not move to that song.

Bill lived galloping, jumping, following the wind from adventure to sex-venture in New York from age sixteen on. He first answered a personal ad. Sex with strangers seemed dangerous to me. That probably sounds judgmental. At the time I was naive and unknowledgeable about homosexual life and hook-ups. My own psychosexual development was firmly stuck in the latency stage.

I once asked him, "Aren't you ever afraid someone will hurt you?"

"Oh, I can read people. Besides, I'm fast, my legs are strong. I could kick someone in the crotch or the throat and be outta there before they know it…besides, these guys are older than me, they're usually high on something… I can get away."

He might as well have announced, "I am invincible!"

Although also a teenager, I felt overcome by parental-type gut reactions I was having to Bill's automatic and convenient guarantees for his personal safety. Yeah, I believed he could read people pretty well, but he was such a know-it-all. He always had an answer. Our worldviews, perceptions, and attitudes differed. He behaved like a typical omnipotent, daredevil teenager. I was the unusual one. I had inherited the shtetl worrying gene, which was reinforced daily in my household. The women in my family programmed me. Even as a young person I often found myself treading water in anxiety, fear, and worst-case expectations. Bill never knew it, but he evoked my internalized grandmother. The grandmother wanted to shut down his cockiness, but I was much more passive than that.

"I worry about you." He laughed and really paid no more attention to what I was saying, just like I never cared to hear the advice or worries of my mother or grandmother. Bill was confident and having the time of his life in a bacchanalian world of drugs and orgies. It fascinated me. Some part of me insanely envied his no-regret, seemingly cost-free pursuits of pleasure—I, a repressed sexual naif, and he, an outlaw getting satisfied.

Rebellious, reckless, and daring as he was, he still paid his own way. He'd achieved that level of maturity. During high school he washed cars, and in college he held a part-time job as a short order cook at, no joke intended, the local Dairy Queen. Bill reaped the benefits of hard work. He could fend for himself. And he knew the streets. He showed me the "hot" bike he'd picked up at Greasy Tony's, a popular local cheesesteak and sub joint that we often frequented in the wee hours after partying.

"I paid seven dollars for it. I just repainted it this sky

blue color. So now the bike can't be identified. It's stuck in fourth gear, but it's getting me around." And so it did: to the train station, the bus station, and school. How thrifty was that?

Two wheels were all Bill could handle though. He was a terrible driver, and never got his license during all the time I knew him. After he initially obtained his learner's permit I experienced two samplings of his driving as a passenger in someone else's vehicle. Both times I prayed for my survival. Subsequently, I decided never to take him out for driving practice, and not to be in a car with him at the wheel. Because he wasn't in control. Though soulful and gracefully rhythmic on the dance floor, his driving reactions were spasmodic and jerky. It was incomprehensible. But, he was so good looking and funny that other girls with crushes on him took him out in their vehicles. I wasn't very surprised when I found out he crashed one girl's car, and knocked out his top four front teeth requiring surgery. That might have been the only time anything had marred his physical beauty.

And now I have to come to a stop, pumping my brakes gently (unlike Bill) so there's not too much jolting. I consider these musings the early developmental era of Bill's and my relationship. Or, I could call it, "Paula and Bill in the Years Before She Came Out."

Our joyous camaraderie liberated and diverted me through adolescence, countering the heaviness of puberty and my anxious household. Lucky for me. At age twenty when I realized I was a lez, I told Bill first. Of course, he had expected my lesbian actualization to happen sooner or later being the gay expert he was. He foresaw it. He accepted me. He understood. He was my anchor. When my dyke door finally unlocked, Bill's door opened wider taking me deeper into his man-loving world—an unbelievable dominion of unlimited sex, drugs, and dance club pulsation.

There's far more for the telling of our companionship, which continued through our twenties. For now, I acknowledge Bill's deep imprint on my young soul, and I revel in vivid memories of our escapades.

Chapter 3

Inspection

You would have thought you were in the Army with a resounding announcement like "Inspection!" I was aware of military routines because I watched a lot of World War II movies with my father. I was nine, and in Mrs. Stearn's fourth grade class at P.S.152 in uptown Manhattan. Yes, that was my teacher's real name, and it proved to be horribly accurate. Mine was the accelerated class, the smartest kids in the fourth grade. Our class was also well-trained, well-behaved, and compliant with authority. Like obedient soldiers we snapped-to when our commander, our teacher, officially called for Inspection first thing on random mornings.

Despite its daily possibility, the event always felt like a surprise attack. Each time I panicked. I dreaded what Inspection entailed and what it revealed, which was very personal information.

Inspection consisted of three checkpoints: fingernails, hair, and the presence of a handkerchief or tissues to use. I was a chronic nail-biter, which was why I cringed when Inspection began. How could I protect myself, hide this weakness? Although my fingernails were not torn and bloodied, they were chewed-down. At each Inspection I worried how Mrs. Stearn would assess them.

My aunt Esther always criticized me for biting my nails which was particularly painful, she being one of the three main women in my life, which included my mother and maternal grandmother. Whenever Esther caught sight of my nails she embarrassed me, although not quite as aggressively as Mrs. Stearn might have. Still, her judgment pierced me.

She once said of my nails, "It's a dead giveaway."

What did it give away about me? That I was an overly nervous youth?

According to Esther, bitten nails were a personality flaw that, if discovered, would somehow deny me future personal and employment success. Winners don't bite their nails. So, when Esther was around I worked to keep my hands out of view. I was continually, unnaturally on guard with her. I maneuvered our conversations away from any topic that I thought would remind Esther to look at my offensive digits. If and when the women in the family started talking about their manicures, I quickly left the room in self-defense.

When I was in my teens, Esther mailed me a postcard, the Venus de Milo, the classic statue of the armless beauty. She wrote, "This is what will happen to you if you keep biting your nails." That was rough. Regardless of her ongoing comments, my nail biting and self-consciousness continued.

There were about ten seconds between Mrs. Stearn's announcement of Inspection and the beginning of the ritual. During that time the class scrambled to borrow tissues from each other. With special folding, the talented were able to make one tissue look like several.

We were required to keep a record of the inspections, a chart of acceptance or rejection. Mine was contained on the back pages of a black and white-speckled University notebook. One column listed the dates of Inspection and another column contained checkmarks, which indicated passing Inspection. There were no eventual rewards or advantages for having an abundance of checks. So far, I had passed every Inspection. Oddly, Mrs. Stearn had not yet honed in on my torn cuticles.

Inspection started with row one. Mrs. Stearn approached the row. Apprehensively, we all stood at attention and presented our hands for examination. Mrs. Stearn moved purposefully down the row, pausing at each desk, first eyeing each student's nails, every single one of which needed to be cut and perfectly cleaned. She scanned each desk for tissues or a handkerchief. Lastly, she carefully considered the neatness of each student's hair, the whole process lasting maybe four seconds. A nod and a smile meant you had achieved the three criteria, and you could sit down.

You'd mark a check in your notebook, and slowly exhale. Relief. Count your blessings! This was the equivalent of the gladiator's thumbs-up moment in the Circus Maximus. You will live for today! Mrs. Stearn proceeded through the five rows, approving or rejecting. There was a gut wrenching price to pay for not meeting the checklist requirements. If she didn't nod, Mrs. Stearn glared at the unprepared student and demeaned her.

I remember a classmate, Robin, who sat diagonally from me in the next row. Robin had coarse, kinky, ash-blond hair of medium length that didn't look easy to control or style. She was a quiet, introverted girl who dressed a bit dowdy, but generally looked fine. One day Mrs. Stearn gave Robin the once over and yelled at the top of her lungs, "Why didn't you brush your hair?" In reality her hair looked no different than any other day. Robin stammered and cowered as she attempted to recover from the verbal blow, her face flaming. The classroom was silent, but Robin's shame was palpable. Little did she know that a bad hair day would be so devastating. What did she or any of us do to deserve such mean treatment?

All the unacceptable ones, the losers, had to remain standing until the end of the review. All looked down at their feet. Public humiliation—Pilgrim style—was their punishment. Scowling for what seemed like eternity, Mrs. Stearn ultimately screamed in her scariest voice, "Sit down! Depending on Mrs. Stearn's decision, a kid might feel brutalized or reborn for the rest of the day. I feared the fate of the condemned.

The magic time was 9:15am. If inspection didn't occur by that time in the morning, it wasn't happening. Darkness immediately dissipated. I cannot describe the peace I felt on non-Inspection days.

Mrs. Stearn, Mrs. Dorothy Stearn. The Merriam-Webster dictionary defines the adjective "Stern" perfectly: "Having a definite hardness or severity of nature or manner. Expressive of severe displeasure." Mrs. Stearn was that force made flesh.

I was awed by her and feared that menacing voice. I didn't want to be on her bad side. I desperately wanted her to like me. She was tall, pretty, shapely, and always dressed impeccably in form-fitting skirts and blouses. She must have been in her thirties, my mother's age. Her high cheekbones and lightly tanned skin made me wonder if she was part Native American. She was no doubt exotic. She ran a strict regime in class and expected a lot from us academically.

When Mrs. Stearn disciplined, I felt sympathy pains for the unlucky classmate. Still, when I described Mrs. Stearn to my mother at the beginning of the school term, I merely said that she was beautiful, and "looks like you." I thought that my mother was attractive, but there was also the element of pleasing her with my statement. The urge to please was a reflex action. My mother returned home from the first parent-teacher conference amused. Over coffee she told my father that Mrs. Stearn was a "mulatto" and recounted my saying that they looked alike.

Why didn't I ever say anything to my parents about Inspection? I was ashamed of my anguish. I didn't have a lot of experience in asking for help when I was troubled. I just didn't believe my parents could comfort me or resolve my situation. I assumed that I was supposed to take care of myself.

I guess Inspection was meant to force us to be properly attired and presentable for school or life, but being on edge about it gave me more reason to bite my nails. Every time I was inspected, I prayed that Mrs. Stearn would just think I cut my nails too short. My good fortune ran out one morning. At a high volume that echoed in my head all day, she exclaimed, "YOU BITE YOUR NAILS!" exposing my weakness, stripping me bare in front of my peers. No nod, no smile, no check, no escape. I joined the ranks of the scorned. The rest of that day was a blur.

Chapter 4

Blue Nevus

A dark-blue or blue-black nevus is a smooth congenital anomaly of the skin formed by melanin-pigmented spindle cells in the lower dermis. The blue color comes from its deeper location in the skin than other nevi. Blue nevi are generally harmless, but they can be mimicked by malignant lesions, aka melanoma.
Merriam-Webster Dictionary

When I was seventeen, I wanted to play basketball at New Brunswick High School and work as a camp counselor during the upcoming summer. I needed medical clearance for both physical endeavors. I was slim, athletic, and healthy, so this was really no big deal.

My mother made an appointment with her idol, Dr. Silverman, our family physician. She considered him a demigod. I don't know exactly when this reverence began. You could never criticize him. If we ever tried, even jokingly, we were quickly shot down with my mother's guilt-inducing stare, which communicated, "You're killing me." And, she'd appear suddenly stricken to prove her point. She looked to Dr. Silverman for advice. Even though they were peers, she treated him like a wise, older member of our extended family. He was Jewish, which gave him instant credibility and meant everything to her. Dr. Silverman was indeed a father figure for my mother. My maternal grandfather died when she was eleven, leaving her with a lifelong yearning for his guidance and attention.

As we drove to the appointment. I imagined my mother and Dr. Silverman catching up in animated conversation sprinkled with Yiddish, me daydreaming while he checked me out.

There was always a delay of at least an hour in the waiting room because Dr. Silverman had a large, loyal following. Everyone wanted ample time with him. I snuggled into my seat in the reception area and shifted my consciousness. When the nurse finally called my name, my mother nudged me to move as I was deep into fantasizing. However, in the examination room after routinely evaluating my temperature, heartbeat, and breathing, Dr. Silverman jolted me out of my state of relaxation. He pointed to the bluish-black mole on my right cheek.

He said most forcefully, "I don't like that!"

What, what, what doesn't he like? What does he mean?

My body stiffened. He frowned as he inspected further, and my anxiety quickly rose, heart hammering against my ribs, my mouth completely dry. My mood had changed instantaneously, going from zero to panic-stricken to the worst-case scenario as I tended to do. Expect the worst! Something terrible was about to be revealed.

The Holocaust left this legacy to my family. It had certain side effects. I became hyper-vigilant at a young age. Adeptly, I could interpret facial expressions and size up body language in our home of limited emotional discussion. One thing was clear. Dr. Silverman had never looked at me this way, nor had he ever spoken to me in such a somber tone. I forced words out of my mouth.

"Why? What's the problem?"

He was taking too long to answer. I cringed as I awaited his response, the atmosphere foreboding. Grasping the edge of the examining table, I sturdied myself, waiting for the blow. In my head there was a drum roll. Dr. Silverman was direct and blunt. "Well, it's a blue nevus. It could develop into a melanoma."

All I heard was, "Blah blah blah MELANOMA." And then a symphony of dismal minor chords played in my head, just like in films when tragedy is anticipated.

Oh, my God! There's a melanoma on my face? That's the worst skin cancer. It's a death sentence.

One might wonder why I was so familiar with this insidious cancer, this monster, melanoma. Since my early days in the school library I was fascinated and terrified by reading about dark subject matter: gruesome diseases, the Nazis, bloody dictators, serial killers, pain, suffering, torture, martyrs, the deaths of the saints. Though riveting, these topics completely unraveled and unnerved me. Now I was literally face to face with a potentially homicidal mole. I felt like the subject of Edvard Munch's painting, *The Scream*.

That damn mole! I wasn't born with it, and I'm not sure when it first developed. It was odd that no one ever questioned its sudden existence, including me, though I was a child. Suddenly, one morning when I awoke, it was just there? Spontaneous generation? I can only surmise the mole birthed when I was in grammar school, according to my school pictures. It appeared in my fourth grade class photo. Why was it bluish-black and not brown like regular moles? Ordinary brown moles were raised above the skin. My multi-colored mark lay flush, its origins well beneath the surface. In junior high school my friend, Cathy, used to comment about it.

"The color of your mole changes according to the color of your clothes—it's like a chameleon!" Cathy saw more hues than blue and black in the mole, especially when I wore red or green plaids. For God's sake! The last thing I wanted in junior high school was attention paid to a freaky facial mark with a diverse color palette. Luckily, Cathy was the only one who really noticed it, and actually admired its peculiar properties.

"What should we do about it, doctor? What's the next step?" I tried to control my nervousness, yet I was also ready for immediate action. Fight or flight? I was trauma-tized by my own dermis. Nothing but discussion of a quick resolution would soothe me. I began to pray silently as I awaited his response. I wasn't a devout Jewish teenager, just the kind that got religious in emergencies.

"We can burn it off here in the office. I'll give you a shot first so it won't hurt. The scar shouldn't be much, like a small circle." Geometrically speaking, that meant a circle with a quarter inch diameter.

Thank you, thank you, thank you, God.

"Bring on the injection," I muttered a little hysterically. My disposition suddenly reversed. Uplifting and victorious major chords trumpeted in my head because there was a solution. I could happily live with a little, flesh-colored, indented circle on my cheek. It might even look cute. Scars have background stories. My father had a facial scar on his upper right cheek, an injury from playing street hockey as a kid. I always considered it appealing, distinctive, and cool. In my case, a small circle seemed a fair trade for the deadly "beauty mark."

Thank goodness Dr. Silverman and I agreed on immediate intervention. He was my hero! Perhaps he deserved the adoration given to him by my mother. The impending demise of the blue nevus would be mourned by no one except...

Though present in the room, my mother had been uncharacteristically silent throughout the examination and discussion of the mole. She, who revered Dr. Silverman, wasn't automatically voicing support for his recommendation. I wouldn't describe her as disengaged, but she wasn't distressed or worried about the mole. This was beyond un-usual. Ordinarily, she worried about everything, paying emotional homage to our shtetl ancestors. Our foremothers believed that worrying warded off evil. There's always something to worry about. The women in my family ex-celled at worrying! My mother should have been way more stressed-out than me, being my anxiety role model and someone who feared cancer.

Maybe she didn't hear or digest Dr. Silverman's warning. Or, had she ignored it? Gone into denial? What was wrong with her? She seemed to be in a different dimen-sion. She stared at the blue nevus fondly like a dear, old friend as Dr. Silverman readied the syringe with a pain-killer. As he wiped my cheek with alcohol she blurted out, "But it's so pretty...perfectly placed on her cheek, exactly where I pencil in my beauty mark. Elizabeth Taylor has one there."

Oh, I get it now. She's mixed up our identities and beauty marks. What the hell! I don't care about cosmetics and beauty marks. This isn't a beauty mark, it's a bad omen. This is a matter of life and death. Does she even know what melanoma is? I won't die for a beautifully positioned, rival mole to Elizabeth Taylor's.

I couldn't believe my mother was waxing poetic and romanticizing the mole. Then another possibility occurred to me. Maybe she feared that my face would be horribly dis-figured by the excision. That would be legitimate, but she never voiced that concern. Regardless, my decision to re-move the mole would not be swayed.

"Okay. Let's do it...NOW!" I was practically begging. I wanted this operation completed.

Then the event occurred. It took less than a minute. A brief odor of burnt skin accompanied the sizzling of the blue nevus. No bloodiness followed. My mother remained skeptical, sad, and disbelieving about the whole process. By the time we left Dr. Silverman's office, me with a Band-Aid on my cheek, I felt mentally exhausted, but also thankful that the mole was gone. My mother was strangely despondent. All over a beauty mark. What about possibly saving my life?

Each day after the mole eradication I examined the spot it once occupied. There was a small circular scab as predicted, which lasted for about a week. I stared at the mirror obsessively. During week two when the scab started to come off, I thought I saw a tiny dot of a blue black area remaining under my skin. It was minute, but was there within the petite circular scar. I analyzed that scar nonstop, maniacally. It should have looked clear. Could it be that a piece of the reviled mole was still lurking? I rushed to my mother.

"I need another appointment with Dr. Silverman. He didn't get all of it. Look!" She inspected my cheek carefully. Apparently, her vision differed from mine.

"It might be part of the scab."

Was she crazy? Why wasn't she scared of me dying? Losing my cool, I yelled, "It is not part of the scab! It's under the skin! Call him!" I wondered whose side she was on, mine or the mole's. She refused to comprehend the danger of the blue nevus, its deviousness. This mole wouldn't let go of me!

At the re-examination appointment Dr. Silverman confirmed that his attempt to burn out the mole had failed. The blue nevus' roots were deeper than anticipated, and so the journey to remove the mole needed to continue. Full excavation required plastic surgery. Dr. Silverman referred me to a local plastic surgeon whose claim to fame was that he had done actress Marlo Thomas' nose.

Dr. Montana was clearly another doctor in great demand. The scene in his crowded waiting room was bizarre. Two types of people filled the seats: patients having gargantuan noses or those with small, ski-lift noses. After several minutes I understood that this was the dichotomy of the "befores and afters" of nose jobs.

I couldn't help but stare at the fascinating nasal evolution. I noticed that the "afters," male and female, weirdly resembled each other. Without DNA manipulation, Dr. Montana had metamorphosed random noses into a community of facial relatives. At a quick glance, this waiting room could've been a family reunion with incestuous bloodlines. I was a little annoyed that I couldn't differentiate myself from the nose people. I wanted a sign saying, "I am not here for my nose. I will not join your clan."

I shouldn't have been surprised, when Dr. Montana completed his examination and commented, "It would be much easier to do your nose." Oh, how he wanted to induct me into his "Stepford" nose army. His presumption that I might want my nose reshaped insulted me. *Just pay attention to the reason we came here, you jerk! It's the mole the MOLE!* Besides, I liked my Schorr nose, and was proud of its distinctive, aquiline nature. My beak! I didn't think it qualified as oversized. Dr. Montana's ski-lift nose was a reconstructed joke, an interpretation of the mainstream's idea of the allegedly perfect proboscis meant for all-around success. After his comment I didn't trust Dr. Montana. From the consult until surgery I worried he would forget the mole, and do rhinoplasty instead.

In an operating room at Saint Peter's Hospital they dosed me with sodium pentathol. While under the anesthesia, Dr. Montana snagged the blue nevus from its sub-dermal level, like removing a torn dandelion root entrenched in the soil. I eventually came to consciousness in the recovery room among the creepy moans and groans of other patients. Despite my drug haze, I had enough awareness to touch my face to make sure my nose hadn't been accidentally altered. Bandages dressed my right cheek, but not my nose.

I had to stay at Saint Peter's Hospital overnight. It wasn't exactly a comfortable experience. Deluged with images of Jesus, Mary, and Saint Peter with every turn of my head, this was the closest I'd ever come to Christian icons. I remembered the first commandment: "Thou shalt have no other gods before Me, nor make unto thee a graven image." Were there other Jewish patients here? Could I relax without guilt in this Catholic environment? That was too much to process in my post-op condition. Without energy to obsess, I conked out.

I woke up quite early the next morning to disturbing sounds and voices. Instead of groans as in the recovery room, I heard a chorus of priests praying in Latin, invoking Jesus. Were they welcoming the dawn or giving last rites? That was enough Christendom for me. I dressed to leave the hospital hours early and waited impatiently for discharge at noon.

My aftercare was simple: follow up with Dr. Montana in two weeks. But, my primary activity was to worry each day about the pathology report. I must have worried well, because the results were clear. No melanoma! The scar was no longer circular, but an inch long line of tissue. Satisfied with my new look, I realized something important about my facial identity. I no longer had the pretty Elizabeth Taylor mole, but I now sported a scar just like my rugged father.

Chapter 5

Coif Formation

(Coif Formation, Coif Firmation)

In the late 1980s, while in my mid-thirties, I allowed my haircutter, Ducki, to coif me with a modified mohawk, a slightly less severe version of the rebellious, punk hairstyle worn mostly by younger men who wanted to stand out and represent. The mohawk began with the Native American Kanienkehaka people of New York State. Traditionally, the hairstyle marked the men responsible for protecting the tribe from invaders. However, the mohawk style never came to be known as a comfort or sign of security in modern America. To varying degrees it expressed alienation from and rejection of the mainstream culture.

Agreeing to any type of radical cut was revolutionary for me, a Capricorn earth sign. This was a seismic change of appearance. Why the extreme shift? Did I desire to become a visually obvious protector of my tribe, the central New Jersey lesbians? Was I seeking to shake up the world's impression of me? Or me of myself? Was disaffection consuming me? Actually, I was depressed and struggling emotionally, caught up in obsessing about my love relationship, which was unraveling as fast as my hair thickened and lost its shape. That and being premenstrual on the day of the haircut caused me to have an aggressive "I don't give a fuck" attitude, and I decided—okay, chop off my hair! Maybe shock treatment would jolt me out of my funk.

After all, I had worn the same hairstyle for over ten years: a naturally curly, short, roundish Jew-fro type creation whose maintenance was pleasantly simple. After a washing I'd dry and gel my hair and then shake my head around to set off an explosion of curls, ready for work or play. I saw no reason to risk a style change. But this initially hip look became stuck.

I'd like to pause here to pay homage to Ducki.

For a decade I denied Ducki a certain freedom by my unreasonably tame and conservative hair decisions. She was known in the New Brunswick community as a talented and innovative stylist among the in-vogue and lesbian crowds. In fact, she probably rehabilitated more Sapphic heads than the local lesbian psychologist. I bet Ducki's success rate rivaled or surpassed said clinician, because a good haircut resuscitated and soothed one's soul. Sometimes the fixing needed was on the outside of the head. A certain snip, the right tint, could lead to emotional release.

Ducki's salon served as an unofficial lesbian information center, be it about community events, concerts, trysts, crushes, or plain old lezzie gossip. The salon provided a neutral space to vent and process the latest episode in one's love life. Ducki ingested a lot of conversation while cutting, which frequently included conflicting versions of events among her clientele couples. Things were hush-hush, though. An agreed-upon imaginary bubble surrounded and protected the confidential, sometimes top-secret discussions between the client and Ducki. The background sounds of music, electric buzzing, hair-washing and blow-drying added layers of privacy. The secondary gain of Ducki's haircare: free peer counseling.

Ducki empathically discussed her romantic struggles too. One caveat though. I made it a point to check out Ducki's mood each time I came for my appointment. I noticed that when things weren't going especially well in her relationship, my haircut was acceptable, but not as carefully fashioned.

In the Old Testament Samson lost his herculean power when his wife, Delilah, betrayed him and ordered a servant to cut off his locks as he slept. In my case, extreme cutting of the locks also posed the risk of vulnerability, the awful weakness of self-consciousness if Ducki went too wild with the shears. Could I trust her? Each time I sat in the salon chair in the past she would ask, "So, what are we doing today?" With some embarrassment, I would reply predictably, restrictively, "You know, the same as last time," and I'd watch her spirit deflate. I was a boring client. I'd blocked her excitement and joie de haircutting by my lack of openness. On some level I felt I owed her.

When I appeared for my haircut appointment that fateful day, Ducki popped the usual question, "What are we doing today?" I heard myself reply, "Whatever you want...whatever you think looks good."

My response jolted her, and she perked up noticeably. I'd surprised both of us! So, aproned and shampooed, I slid, panicked, into the swivel chair anticipating something like a roller coaster ride. But everything happened much faster. In only seconds the situation became irreversible. In the mirror I watched my jaw drop as my image underwent a major transformation, clumps of tresses falling everywhere as Ducki strategically circled my head. The noisiness of the buzzer and the radius of hair spread over the floor reminded me of a sheep shearing I once saw at a craft fair.

I was stunned as I examined the closely shaved sides of my head. Well, no doubt I'd feel cooler in the summer. I comforted myself. My hair would eventually grow back and I could wear a bandana for as long as I felt uncomfortable. However, the end result astounded me, cutting edge and not too far out there. Although I wondered what my county government coworkers would think, I absolutely loved my mohawk, which showcased the distinctive qualities of my hair.

Ducki had lived up to her reputation as a genius with the electric clipper and a visionary with my curly, wavy mane. She had not only re-sculpted my hair, she'd whizzed and whirred my whole being. This was a spiritual event. I felt excited, revitalized, metamorphosed, reborn with a new chic toughness to encounter the world. A therapy session never brightened my aura that much. I strutted out of the salon that day with a fresh attitude. The mohawk marked the beginning of a sacred trinity in my life: me, my hair, and the magical buzzer.

I'd yearned for straighter hair in high school. Back then, having long, "poker-straight" hair was an ideal to be realized. Girls commonly ironed their hair to achieve and ensure that look. Curly styles were unknown, unexplored. One worked to undermine, disempower, and eliminate curls. I always had curly, wavy, and slightly coarse hair, thanks to my Ashkenazi gene pool.

I wasn't so thankful as a teen though. When my hair grew to chin-length, a few haughty cheerleaders, self-assigned arbiters of social acceptance, criticized me for having frizzy hair on humid and rainy days. I succumbed to the pressure. Their judgment drove me to try the product, Curl Free. My younger sister, Laurie, was already using this concoction with success, having received the anti-curl message from her junior high school peers. An odorous liquid hair relaxant, Curl Free left hundreds of split ends in its path as it straightened, which attested to the potency of its chemistry. Some of my individual hairs had well over twenty splits, which was both remarkable and concerning.

Despite the appealing smell of the post-treatment

cream rinse, I wondered what this mixture was doing to my head? Was it safe? Whatever the case, a new door of opportunity had opened for my self-mutilation rituals. I could now choose to split hairs or bite my nails when I felt nervous, bored or restless. In Biology, English, World History I'd split as the particular teacher babbled on endlessly. Although eye-straining, this activity turned out to be hypnotic and meditative with class time elapsing more quickly.

Through my first years of college, the early '70s, I let my hair grow down to my shoulders. I said goodbye to Curl Free, and pursued the opposite route, a wild Janis Joplin hippy look. Though liberated from the social constraints of high school, my hair demanded more complex care. Long, thick and shaggy with thousands of acquired split ends, that mop had a life of its own. We carried on strenuous battles around its day-to-day arrangement.

After a washing my hair defied efforts to dry. Initially, I tried rolling and clipping my hair around large, empty, juice and veggie cans. They had replaced old-fashioned rollers as a homestyle way to dry and shape hair. I borrowed this method from Laurie, whose hair was thick, but not as massive as mine. Then I would bake my head for over three hours under the hair dryer set at its highest temperature. At the expiration of this chunk of time, the hair wrapped around the juice cans was still damp. Unbelievable! I wasn't going to stay under that torturous dryer all day. Frustrated, I was forced into a primitive solution. From that point on I wove two braids after showering, and just left my hair that way. I slept and woke with those braids. It took days for most of the moisture to evaporate, but it is also possible that my hair never completely dried. Upon undoing the braids, I would brush my hair vigorously—a competitive wrestling match against my head and a series of stubborn knots. Many days I cried uncle and gave up.

Back then, I parted my hair in the middle and brushed both sides firmly back to be held by a super-giant hair clip. This clip was one-of-a-kind in its ability to handle the weight and pull of my insistent hair. One of my friends said that the effect of the clip was to make my tightly wound head resemble a durable helmet.

Unfortunately, one day I lost the special clip at the beach while frolicking in the Atlantic Ocean. The pressure of containing my hair while I dove under breaking waves must have been too much. I frantically searched for the clip in the surf, which rapidly became ridiculous. The currents had already taken away my precious accessory, perhaps to a needy mermaid. The loss of the clip became an ongoing dilemma. No clip I subsequently purchased worked as effectively.

During college, I worked part-time in a W. T. Grant department store, which, shortly before the company's bankruptcy, added a beauty parlor for shoppers. Business decisions such as this probably contributed to W. T. Grant's eventual insolvency.

The salon manager had seen me many times with

my Janis Joplin do, and repeatedly proclaimed he could create a beautiful style for me. He kind of stalked my head. I was wary. He didn't exude hipness or any other stereotypical characteristics of the beautician. I thought—who gets their hair done in a W. T. Grant department store? But. after a few weeks I changed my mind. My hair remained wild and unmanageable. I also felt low emotionally, glum and numb around an unfulfilled romantic attraction.

I accepted the manager's proposition because I really didn't give a shit about anything that particular day. I entered the salon, and said, a bit sarcastically, that I was ready to test his claim. The salon was of course not busy, so he took me right away. He cut the length of my hair roughly, and put the cuttings in a plastic bag for me to keep as a souvenir. The end of a phase. I'm not sure what I was supposed to do with the dead hair, or how long I was supposed to keep it. Then the unexpected happened. This formerly unimpressive salon manager possessed amazing skills. He seemed to know my hair intimately. He gave me the shag, a trendy, short, low maintenance style, which celebrated my coarse and resilient locks. Days of high humidity would no longer hold me hostage to frizz anxiety. Bye, bye burden! Now mugginess would enhance my abundant curls. With no more marathon drying, no more split ends, and no need for muscle-bound clips, the shag returned my hair to health. It also totally upped my self-image. I loved my natural attributes more. The shag was a turning point. I vowed never to grow long hair again. The only problem was that I needed a new stylist since W.T. Grant went out of business.

By my mid-forties, post-mohawk, I felt brave enough to experiment on myself and leave Ducki behind. I was fairly certain my strong, springy curls could survive an amateur haircut. I purchased a Wahl electric hair clipper with its numerous attachments for different lengths of buzz. With a bandana as my tiny security blanket and backup, I set out to design and execute my own hairdos using my mohawk as a reference point. Hairdos require maintenance every six weeks to keep looking sharp, an expense that must be figured into the budget. With my new buzzer I could and did save hundreds of dollars annually.

The electric clipper was a plaything with which I actualized one major hair fantasy: to wear a crew cut. Although there is a bit of drag-king in me, I have my father to blame for this particular dream. Laurie and I begged him to let his hair and sideburns grow, but he rigidly sported a crew cut his whole life. However, of his two daughters, I was the butch and internalized him more. I witnessed the haircare and temperature relief his buzzed head brought him. Escape from the summer's dog days existed. So, prior to attending the Michigan Womyn's Music Festival one August, I buzzed my hair to crew cut length with the number two attachment, the second shortest. It wasn't a Marine buzz, but it's androgyny contented me. I expected positive reinforcement from my festival sisters.

Before my journey westward, I stopped at my parents' house to pick up a wheelbarrow for camping. My father, the only one home, answered the door. He was the first to regard my crewcut. I have always resembled my father. I knew I'd inherited his nose. Now I wore his hairstyle. We looked at each other and fell into hysterical laughter. Our boundaries loosened. We were one, we were twins, reflections without a mirror. We continued to chuckle as I loaded the wheelbarrow in my truck, but we didn't speak. Words could not express the mix of shock and glee we shared.

For the past thirty plus years I have sampled and tried on different combinations of waves, curls, and buzzing. I have not once resorted to scarves or hats to hide my handiwork. I do, however, follow one rule: the shorter the haircut, the larger the earrings worn. The earrings assist at times as gender identifiers.

You might wonder how society has responded to my haircuts. Years of intermittent field-participant research have led to the following demographic observation: Black women of all ages favor my buzz styles over every racial, age, and gender group. This statistic is significant!

Although a research minor in grad school, I wasn't pursuing another project. I totally stumbled onto my data. Being hair-radical as a middle-aged woman rarely attracted conversation or reaction from white mainstream men or women. Whether this silence came from people's politeness, distaste, disapproval, or none of the above doesn't matter—I wasn't seeking endorsements.

I'm not sure when or where I encountered my first hair compliment, which happened to be from a Black woman. I remember thanking her and chatting that I buzzed it myself. I wanted to promote hair self-care, its ease, its financial gains. I started to pay more attention over time after receiving praise from five or six other Black women. The individuals and circumstances varied. I recall a government worker at a conference I attended in Trenton taking a break from her duties to talk hair with me. While at Asbury Park City Hall to pick up a civil union certificate, a woman approached me to laud my cut. Once visiting my mother at Robert Wood Johnson Hospital, a woman I estimated to be in her seventies, a church lady, came over to me in the hallway to inquire about my hair. The woman at the deli counter in Stop and Shop admired my latest buzz. Now she treats me like an old friend as she slices and measures the ham and cheese. All Black women.

My research was descriptive and definitely informal. But, there were two ironic constants: randomness and unpredictability. People voluntarily complimented my hair in random locations at random times.

I am sixty nine, and the pattern continues. Last week in the Rite Aid parking lot, a woman stopped her car to tell me she loved my hair. At a recent dental visit the receptionist affirmed my curls. The kudos delights me, and makes me feel multi-culti. Secure in my coif, I can't wait to face the cheerleaders at my next high school reunion.

Chapter 6

The Emergence of Rockin' Bad Paula

My alter-ego, Rockin' Bad Paula (RBP), the lesbian rapper, birthed at age thirty-six in 1989 when hip-hop music dominated the radio waves, and I attended the Rutgers Graduate School of Social Work. This persona developed parallel to my master's research project which studied the relationship between internalized homophobia and self-esteem in lesbians. RBP appeared on the scene as a statistically significant embodiment of the findings and a symbol of my further self-actualization as a dyke. Let me explain.

In 1987 I took a leave of absence from my employment as a probation officer in the conservative entity known as the county court system. Straightville! Although I never completely closeted myself at work, I didn't feel the ease to openly discuss my everyday activities. For example,

I didn't talk about a very important part of my life, the Lesbosonic Funk Force, my dyke rock band.

Even though county workers received state-mandated "cultural sensitivity" training, the band moniker might likely have scared the mainstream listener. The very prefix, "lesbo," was known to cause a reaction. I didn't care to witness the response. So I eliminated lesbian-related conversation from my work socializing which left mostly superficial topics. Partially censoring myself took effort, one cost of internalized homophobia. Gay acceptance had only progressed by inches back then, and I altered my personal sharing according to the particular milieu.

But less than a mile away from the courthouse lay a gentler institution, the Rutgers Graduate School of Social Work (GSSW) where the mission called for working to help uplift and ameliorate the lives of oppressed peoples. I looked forward to entering a setting where my sexual orientation would most likely not be the object of gossip, raised eyebrows, derision, or explanation. Respect!

The grad school offered an opportunity to come out further and live more freely. Sounds great. But first I had to check myself and labor to undo the ingrained self-restriction and omissions I practiced while working for the court the previous twelve years. Now I could retire from hiding and be a true, more vibrant self. I knew this transition would take resolve and consciousness.

A beautiful synchronicity struck me at Rutgers GSSW. I was studying direct practice but agreed to become a research minor solely because I got to select the subject matter. Easy enough. I picked lesbians, which happened to be a population lacking much investigation at that time. Why shouldn't I enjoy my academic efforts with passion and devotion? This was a dream come true— digging into dyke behavior, and focusing on my people. All out in the open! The universe was infusing my soul with lesbianity. I guess I'd been starved for more of it.

First, I had to acquire my professor's approval for my project. That was nerve-wracking. I was afraid and apprehensive because I knew I would have to come out to her during our discussion of my proposed hypotheses. It seemed ridiculous not to. Really, who other than a lesbian would be doing dyke research?

I had never come out to a professor, though. I suffered from those societally induced negative expectations. But I'd made that vow of realness to myself. My inner judge reminded me of that incessantly, so there was no escape. That judge didn't shut up.

I arrived at my professor's office. I felt antsy. After some small talk ensued, it was time for the revelation. Sweating profusely, embarrassing wet stains at the armpits of my shirt. I blurted out without flair,

"Well, you know I'm a lesbian..."

Feeling like an idiot, I shrunk temporarily in place, but my professor just listened. No startle response on her part, just intentness. Did she already suspect I was a lesbian? She didn't act surprised or uncomfortable. I kept searching her face for a clue. I detected no rejection. Coming out clearly rocked my world more than hers. All she cared about were the details of my proposal, so I proceeded to announce my hypotheses.

> 1) *There is a positive correlation between membership in lesbian-identified groups/ organizations and higher self-esteem.*

> 2) *There is a negative correlation between membership in lesbian-identified groups/organizations and internalized homophobia.*

> 3) *Self-esteem is negatively correlated with internalized homophobia.*

That meeting with the professor was a lesson. No repercussions occurred. My internally homophobic fears were met with nothing but support and encouragement. No blame, no shame. My self-esteem glowed a little more brightly. These research professors didn't care who or what you studied, as long as evidence for social work practice was uncovered.

I loved driving around and dispersing my research questionnaires. I dropped my surveys at sites of lesbian gathering: women's bookstores, softball games, a friendly hair salon, women's centers, all great opportunities for schmoozing and making new contacts. Kind of like speed-dating. Every week in research class we reviewed the progress of my study and those of my classmates. It seemed I was much more excited about my work than the others, who were not progressing much with their plans. As a result, the topic of lesbians predominated our class discussions. This was probably the most my peers ever heard or verbalized the word "lesbian" in their lives. Do lesbians do this? Are lesbians like that?

The project set the scene for Rockin' Bad Paula. RBP was a proud, tough-ass androgynous lesbian performer kickin' it in Doc Martens. She wore a beatnik beret, jeans or cutoffs, a tank top, and sunglasses so you couldn't see her eyes. She wanted to be viewed as a woman who took no crap, but she suffered from some stage fright. RBP didn't want that known by the audience. It would have interfered with her self-assured image. The shades provided some kind of power and protection. A few shots of vodka beforehand delivered courage. RBP was brazen, she was blunt, and she was unapologetic. She was bad!

RBP's braggadocio accented her rapping skills and sexual appetite just like the other hip-hop stars, and most importantly, her right to exist as a lesbian! A long percussion introduction played as RBP swaggered onto the stage, her dance moves to the beat, sensuality pronounced. Rappers have natural rhythm, and RBP demonstrated hers before hitting the mic.

In her 1989 hit, "I'm a Lesbian" with the Lesbosonic Funk Force, performed for the lesbian organization, "More Than You Can Count," she introduced and defined herself to the community.

"I'm a member of a group that's one-in-ten
I'm a woman-loving woman, I'm a lesbian
I'm Rockin' Bad and I rap to dykes
Other deejays drop their mics
They fear me when they hear me
Straight deejays don't come near me
But I don't care 'cause I'm self-aware
Society better be prepared! Huh!

My lesbian sexuality is a reality
I am not concerned with causality
I'm shedding my chains when I'm out on the street
I'm wearing my lavender and rockin' to the beat. Huh!

Women, they excite me, they delight me
I want them nightly
Date me, stimulate me
I wish that they would copulate me! Huh!

CHORUS:
I'm rockin', I'm rockin', I'm shockin', I'm a lesbian
I'm rockin', I'm rockin', I'm shockin', I'm a lesbian
I'm rockin', I'm rockin', I'm shockin', I'm a lesbian
I'm rockin', I'm shockin', don't you wanna rock with me?

Women, they excite me, they delight me
I want them nightly

Mate me, gyrate me
I wish that they would copulate me! Huh!

CHORUS

Our band's gigs were usually sign-interpreted. I definitely appreciated the interpreter's signing of "copulate me," which all of our band members learned immediately.

As for the research project, I only proved one hypothesis: that lesbians belonging to lesbian-identified groups/organizations scored lower in levels of internalized homophobia. Self-esteem was not that measurably black and white. My study failed to address the grayer zones, for example, lesbians who consciously compartmentalized their outness from concerns for emotional, professional, and even physical safety. Those partially closeted situations did not necessarily reflect a loss of self-esteem and might be the result of wise choices.

Nevertheless, RBP rapped on at New York City, Philly, and New Jersey pride celebrations, private parties, fundraisers, and other lesbian-identified events. The deceleration of internalized homophobia and the declaration of dyke solidarity powered the performances. In 1994 at "Lesbopalooza" with the band, Ovareaction, RBP announced her election bid for the highest office of the land with the song, "Lesbian President." Why not ponder the possibilities? The rap humorously harkened back to the days of crystal power and worship of the Goddess.

Beneath the Surface

If I were lesbian president,
I certainly wouldn't be hesitant
I'd do away with atom bombs,
My army would be led by Amazons
Instead of minuteman missiles,
I'd shower the country with loads of crystals
The color of the White House would be changed
The Oval Office would be renamed to
The Ova Office where policy is made with
Incense, candles, lotsa rituals

If I were lesbian president
I certainly wouldn't be reticent
The Congress would be disbanded
The legislature would be commanded
By a female consciousness-raising group
With uniforms and badges like a Girl Scout troop
And my policy on pollution?
Clean it up or pay
That's my solution.
We're separating the church and state
You wanna worship the moon?
I can relate.

With my First Lady Lezzie at my side
I'd rule this country with woman-loving pride
My campaign promises would be modest
I pledge allegiance to the Goddess!

If I were lesbian president
I certainly wouldn't be penitent
We gotta change the dominant culture
Get rid of the capitalist vulture
And if you think what I'm saying
Is a lot of jive
Register to vote!
Keep the party alive
The condition of the country is really a mess
The more I think about it, more I stress
We got to get this nation out of traction
And we're doing it here with Ovareaction!

It has been thirty years plus since "Lesbian President" debuted. As of this writing, numerous LGBTIQ people have been elected to represent their districts, which is a beautiful thing. Can the presidency be within reach this century?

Now a white-haired crone, RBP has reappeared intermittently as a solo act to wave the lesbian banner and be a voice of self-liberation. She is available to facilitate the lessening of internalized homophobia. There are mantras she teaches for a dyke to utilize in a self-hypnotic kind of way, a home study course. The chorus of "I'm a Lesbian"— "*I'm rockin', I'm rockin' I'm shocking...*" is one popular chant of self-love. RBP knows coming out is a life-long process for which **society better be prepared!** I say to myself, "Preach on it, Rockin' Bad!" The message is still so necessary.

Acknowledgments

My gratitude goes out to all of the sisters in my reading squad: Joanne Fuccello, Brad Lyon, Kay Turner and most importantly, my main triad, Barbara E. Milton, Jr., Kay Osborn, and my first cousin, Reese Shamansky. How could I go wrong with such a learned crew?

Major props to Barb Pritchard, who designed the book cover which we birthed together. She captured the colors and images spinning around in my brain.

Of course, I am indebted to my spouse, Karen Siegel, who listened to these stories a million times, each time with renewed interest, and supported me all the way.

About the Author

Born in 1953, Paula Schorr spent her formative years in the Dyckman Valley of Manhattan before relocating to New Jersey as a pre-teen. She grew up being told she would be a teacher, but she defied that prediction and randomly became a probation officer through a federal job program. For the next thirty three years she supervised and investigated convicts, juvenile delinquents, and did crisis intervention work with teens and their families. She also learned a great deal about the "others" in society. She obtained her MSW from the Rutgers School of Social Work in 1989, and her clinical license a few years later.

With Gemini rising in her astrological chart there is a duality to her nature. In her other life she has been a musician and out performer since 1973 when she first sang at women's liberation parties with the lesbian a cappella group, The Oral Tradition. A dabbler playing tenor sax, rhythm and bass guitars, she co-founded and sang with the bands Slip of the Tongue, Mothra, Lesbosonic Funkforce, Fertile Crescent, and Ovareaction, the latter doing original music.

Paula aka "Rockin' Bad Paula," claims to have been the first lesbian rapper in Middlesex County, New Jersey.

GREEN HEART
LIVING
— PRESS —

Green Heart Living Press publishes inspirational books and stories of transformation, making the world a more loving and peaceful place, one book at a time.

You can meet Green Heart authors on the Green Heart Living YouTube channel and the Green Heart Living Podcast.

www.greenheartliving.com

Made in the USA
Middletown, DE
06 April 2023